Pag 39 Be

NEWPORT AT WORK

JAN PREECE

AMBERLEY

To my dear wife Sally and my six children: Jody, Toria, Lucy, Anna, Gemma and Jan.

To Duncan, and to my dear friend Joasia.

And to the hardworking men and women of Newport past.

First published 2019

Amberley Publishing
The Hill, Stroud
Gloucestershire, GL5 4EP

www.amberley-books.com

Copyright © Jan Preece, 2019

The right of Jan Preece to be identified as the Author
of this work has been asserted in accordance with the
Copyrights, Designs and Patents Act 1988.

ISBN 978 1 4456 8633 2 (print)
ISBN 978 1 4456 8634 9 (ebook)

British Library Cataloguing in Publication Data.
A catalogue record for this book is available
from the British Library.

Origination by Amberley Publishing.
Printed in the UK.

CONTENTS

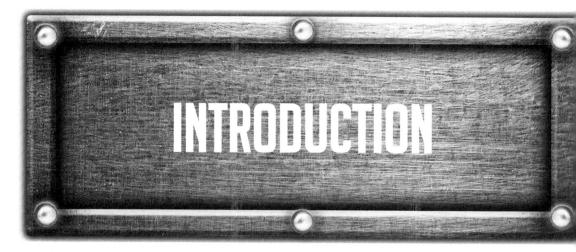

INTRODUCTION

'Work' is an ambiguous word. While it describes the act, it doesn't really consider the sentiment behind it. Is it a depressing daily drudgery, a man pumping the same handle for forty years just to watch yet another drab component dropping into the wire cage? Or is it the actions of the fifty-year-old nuclear physicist, deliriously happy because he gave up his lucrative career to fulfil a lifetime's ambition to become a paper boy? Whatever, we are all engaged in it, in some way or other – supporting our families or supporting ourselves. We all need to work at some point.

Newport at Work is the story of both the town and the city – of then and of now – from the early trades, the running and the upkeep of the castle, through generations of growth, change and new beginnings. This is not a book about statistics, and sadly space does not allow the mention of the hundreds of Newport companies who offered employment to the community. Instead, it concerns the type of work we once did, the heydays and the decline, and a look to the future and the 'new' industries.

Sprawling Newport from the Transporter Bridge.

The list is long and varied. Being a major port, through time Newport has dealt with most commodities – in the raw state and man-made. It is a manufacturing base and it is also a hub of communication and distribution through its large docks complex.

Over 300 years Newport has gone through the whole spectrum. From market town to industrial giant, through the Depression and then the hard climb back through a maze of new technologies, while accepting modernity and the true core of the city and its history.

In welcoming the modern commercial landscape a balance has to be struck and sympathy shown to the fine Victorian architecture of the centre, and at the same time finding a useful outcome for the empty shops and upper-floor offices and storage apartments that were once part of the commerce of the city.

Newport at Work highlights the growth and decline of the city as an industrial force and examines commerce and work, both new and old, in all its variations. Thanks to the members of the Newport community who have shared their experiences and memories, and a part of their lives.

No more coal hoists. A modern crane deals with this shipment of foreign coal.

THE FISHING VILLAGE

THE FOUNDATIONS FOR A CITY

Whereas the titles Novus Burgus, New Castle and Castle Town give a broad indication on the origins of Newport as we currently know it, local historian Scot mentions that Newport was once called Pentre Govian, which means 'Blacksmiths Village'. The reference to ironworking has certainly stayed, as has Fisherman Lane, both suggesting a link with two defined industries.

Ironworks, foundry and steel making were all principal industries from the mid-1700s. Fishing has also played its part in the commerce of the city, mostly due to salmon, the king of fish. During this period prior to industrialisation, the river and its estuarial waters would have been relatively clean, as compared to the river that most of us remember, being filled with the spoils of the coal and iron trades. Fisherman Lane was found to be adjacent to the castle, next to the Fish Store in Shaftesbury, and originally was the approach to the ford that was once the river crossing. This was to be found under the present road bridge. On the east bank it linked

Pleasure and work on the Usk at Newport.

with the steep climb up to Christchurch, passing over Akeman Street (Christchurch Hill), and was one of the ancient routes to London.

On the west bank the 'road', if it could be called that, would have passed through a sunken cutting lined with trees, passing through what is now known as Pentonville and proceeding, via

Christchurch Road. In ancient times this was Akeman Street, a principal route between the village of Newport and Christchurch.

The ford crossing the river was directly under the present town bridge, which was built because of the hard riverbed at the time.

an ancient highway called the 'British Road', to what is now Barrack Lane and then to Basseleg. Pentonville was derived from the Saxon Pyndan.

Ancient Britons, it would appear, were more than capable of executing major engineering projects and the British Road, as opposed to the Roman road, was one such achievement.

And it has been further suggested this ancient settlement built on the shore of the Usk had some major significance long before that of Caerleon.

Prior to the castle being built, the miller, blacksmith and the nail maker would have been the principal sources of trade in the village. The mill was a necessity. The oldest industry in Newport was undoubtably Saxon as the flour mill in Shaftesbury enjoyed a lineage of nearly 1,000 years, equalled only by St Woolas Cathedral.

The importance of this area, originally known as Pendan, cannot be understated as in 1500 BC it was a major seat of administration. Mill Street and its surrounds are steeped in history: it is a boundary line for the old town, a principal route through the village and a medieval centre of government.

The mill, whose stones would have been obtained from the quarry at Barrack Fields or at Basseleg Road, which had a large mill pond that was originally next to a tidal pill, and much later the Monmouthshire Canal. The miller was a very important person. He would have been moderately well-off, but often prone to hostilities during times of riots and bread shortages. The mill building would have been owned by the lord of the manor, who would have been paid a fee for the use of the mill.

Meanwhile, the blacksmith, the miller and the nail maker provided the nucleus of trade and work in the pre-Norman village. Not forgetting food production and the making of garments and so forth. It would appear that the ancients excelled in their work with iron – something that has

Brynglas House, once the home of industrialist J. J. Cordes. The red-brick secton was a later addition, as was the school hall.

The original residence and the only evidence of the Dos works are the preserved cottages, on the site of the original works.

never left the city. In the nineteenth century the Dos Nail Works was founded and, as late as the 1960s, the Healey and Peart Company produced nails in their factory adjacent to Caerleon Road.

The Dos Ironworks was the first major works in Newport. It was built by the Spanish industrialist J. J. Cordes, who in later years lived in Brynglas House. This became Brynglas Secondary Modern School and is still intact and now used as learning centre.

THE ROMAN INFLUENCE

When the Romans came it heralded a new era. The Britons, who were described as 'uncountable' owing to their numbers, gravitated to the Roman cities, of which Caerleon was uppermost in importance. The Roman society of baths, shops and numerous garrison barracks changed the climate in terms of work, the manufacturer of good and supply.

The society that the Romans brought would have opened up a world of new possibilities for commerce and trade. They didn't arrive on a Eurolines bus, they were an invading force, epitomised by their massive boundary walls and garrison towns. However, like it or not they were here for hundreds of years and left their mark in many agreeable ways.

Any prominence in administration was lost to Caerleon, and Newport fell into the doldrums. The land became a war-ridden melting pot of uncertainty. The Britons were hopelessly ill-equipped to deal with life outside the Roman Empire. And so it remained until the arrival of the Normans.

The Roman amphitheatre at Caerleon. On a distant hill is the village of Christchurch, which the ancient road to London passed through.

Caerleon, a Roman garrison town and a once thriving port.

THE NORMANS AND AFTER

Newport's first castle was a wooden stockade, and this was evidence that the old ancient outpost was becoming a garrison. Prior to around AD 1090 castles were built of wood, and after that date, of stone. At that time Newport had a population of around fifty and was still very much the fishing village.

The Bell Inn, a seventeenth-century coaching inn in Caerleon, close to the river and the quayside.

The Roman occupation and the ensuing years undoubtably meant Newport's progression from a village to a borough, and now to a city, took longer than it may have done otherwise. For a period of nearly 400 years Caerleon had stolen the advantage from Newport. This continued through the centuries, as Caerleon was a dock of importance and remained as such in spite of the wars and other period of unrest that prevailed.

It was the canals and the improving berthing facilities Newport offered that led to the demise of the shipping trade in Caerleon. Working life in Newport, being as the name suggests, a port, has always been linked to the sea and in particular ship repair and shipbuilding.

With the first castle or stockade came a new demand from the limited workforce. Arrowheads, bows, quivers and building skills were then required to arm those charged with the security of the camp. The castle, which is suggested was a Norman motte, was possibly constructed by William Rufus around 1075; however, Newport Castle as we know it today was built in the fourteenth century.

It is worth a moment to ask where did such a small population's skills originate? Building castles, which took many years, required a new dimension in the workforce. The stonemason, to name but one craftsman, would have been of prime importance and the amount of physical labour required to construct the massive walls and arches would have been considerable.

In addition, what were the workforce requirements to service a castle and the troops, or whoever was in residence at the time. The nobility had their own servants. In addition, there existed the steward or major (Domo), the highest person in the household staff. The constable was responsible for the horses, grooms and pages, while the marshal was engaged in all military matters. The chamberlain was one who was charged with the management of the household, both domestic and financial, while clothing and some other domestic matters were left to the master of the wardrobe.

With so many involved in the logistics of everyday life, it is difficult to imagine that Newport had population of just fifty. Perhaps just those who resided and worked outside the castle walls were counted?

EARLY SHIPBUILDING

Geographically, being on the water's edge, Newport's workforce would inevitably lean towards matters of the sea. Shipbuilding and ship repair would account for a significant number of workers engaged in that branch of heavy industry. In 1847, while in the throes of the Industrial Revolution, Scott, in his *History of Newport*, lists just three shipbuilders: 'Nicolas and Cooke near the Town Bridge. Willmet and Hall, The Dry Dock. Young and Cook, Rodney Warf'.

There were five sailmakers all trading in the town, but in comparison an inordinate number of straw-bonnet makers – a total of thirteen in all. Perhaps it was pleasure craft that were on the slips at that point.

What constitutes a ship or boat builder is a matter of conjecture. Would a shipwright turning out two or three fishing smack a year constitute an entry in a trade directory? It is unlikely that any legislation existed to prevent the individual building and launching of a boat. So, there is a high possibility that the number of boat builders on the Usk were greater in number than the directories state.

Considering the evidence brought to light at the discovery of the *Newport Medieval Ship*, it is clear that the ship repair and building industry played a prominent part in the story of work in Newport. The *Newport Medieval Ship*, a sizeable vessel, was moored for what is thought to be repairs and possible refit on the site of the recently built arts centre.

Loading from the east bank. Was this early engraving the *Tredegar Boat* or the *Moderator Boat*, whose landing stage was on the opposite bank.

Timbers of the *Newport Medieval Ship*, discovered on the town reach while groundwork for the new arts centre was being laid.

" Vivian Jolliffe," Screw Tug built by Messrs. Mordey, Carney & Co., Ltd.

Pictured in the Old Town Dock is the screw tug *Vivian Jolliffe*, built by Mordey and Carney.

NEWPORT'S CHARTERS

The charter bestowed on the town by James I in 1624 presents a fascinating insight into the Newport of the future. The ordinances set out and highlighted the rules of trade and occupancy of buildings and stalls relating to business and the markets of the day. It offered protection from strangers or foreigners setting out a stall, to matters of health and safety. 'No person shall wash clothes or garments within 12 feet of any well.' A fine of 12*d* (1s) would be paid to the town for each offence.

On first reading, the charters had the benefit of Newport townsfolk very much in mind. They were complicated yet protective to the town's community. Names synonymous to the present-day city were appearing in places of importance – the Morgans and the Herberts to name but two. It was as if the stage was being set to cope with the massive changes about to manifest in the form of the impending Industrial Revolution.

It was illegal for any person to sell fish – salmon, sewen, flook, bordshed or sole – before it was presented at the Market House. Here it would remain for a period of an hour while it was inspected by officers, before being sold or offered to the public.

Brewers and those producing ales to be sold were required 'for every barrel of ale to produce one Kilderkin of good small wort' for the poor to have drink. I can't recall that law ever being rescinded!

The concept of Newport being a fishing village is an interesting one. The name Usk derives from an early Brittonic word meaning 'abundant in fish'. The salmon has certainly been prized

A small craft leaves the port, set against the backdrop of the City Bridge.

throughout history. However as for a fishing fleet being based here for the purpose of extracting fish from the sea, that is highly debatable. Yet, prior to the Industrial Revolution and the mining of coal, etc., the waters would have been relatively clean. The lower reaches of the Usk are deep and wide and even in the most polluted days, when heavy industry was at its zenith, many species of saltwater fish were to be found in the river, which is really at its widest point estuarial. Recent surveys on the state of the seabed in the lower reaches, identified many species, including the twaite shad, a member of the herring family, though not used as a food fish since the 1800s. The Usk is one of only four rivers in Britain where this historic fish spawns

Newport has always stood on marshland, and before the days of land reclamation much of the old town would have been almost surrounded by the waters that swept across the flat terrain. Fishing and hunting for wild animals would have probably been the chosen option as a food source because of the watery landscape – hence the adopted name of the 'Fishing Village'.

Early engravings show small single sail craft in and around the castle, no doubt using the water gate. There is, however, a train of thought suggesting the traditional coracle might have been used on the Usk in the lower reaches. I can only think that the tiny craft would have been impractical in the fast-running tidal waters, but it would have been perfect in the marshy waters that almost surrounded the castle and part of the village.

THE INDUSTRIAL REVOLUTION

Our story of work in Newport is set against a backdrop of Civil War and insurrection, all of which has been well documented. The presence of the castle, the river crossing and the inherent skill of the small population provided the impetus to a massive period of growth during what was known nationally as the Industrial Revolution.

The Cordes Ironworks was the first major industrial enterprise in Newport and was built in 1835. It was constructed on the banks of the Monmouthshire Canal and quite near to the Crindau Pill, which was at one time listed as 'Malpas Dock'.

The canal was split into two arms – the junction can be seen at Malpas and is directly under the M4 flyover. Hundreds of navvies were employed in bringing the canal to Newport. Hard-living men and their families, many of whom no doubt stayed in the town. The operating companies, initially those who financed the cut, and then the Great Western Railway and their paying customers, all contributed to the workforce created by the coming of the canal.

The much-mentioned Union Inn of Lower Dock Street, which became the Richmond Hotel and then the River View Club, became a benchmark in the canal's history. It was recorded that the inn shone a bright light that could be seen at a distance and was the point of reference for those hundreds of navvies crossing the dangerous marshland to the ground works, which would become the canal. Where, I wonder, are those precious records that would give us an insight into the revenue gained from the workforce engaged in that mammoth undertaking?

Navvies in that period could earn, in today's money, around 25p a day. Those engaged with the railways found their wages were often slow in arriving and were frequently paid out in an adjoining pub or inn. The canal companies probably had the same practices in place, which gave the Union Inn a ready-made clientele in addition to being an iconic point of light from which the navvies sourced their place of work. Nice work if you could get it.

The practice of using a local hostelry as the paymaster's office continued into the twentieth century. Here in Newport dockers often were paid from the Waterloo Hotel, a large Victorian pub at the gates of the Alexandra Docks.

Hanna Griffith founded Griffith's Clothiers from her front room in 1870. She made flannel shirts for local navvies, and it is of no surprise that by the early 1900s her company was one of the largest in South Wales, employing hundreds of people. She was quite obviously an entrepreneur who saw a huge market from the workmen engaged in constructing the canals and the docks. It was even more remarkable that it was a woman at the helm, which was not the norm for that period in our history.

A Victorian lantern slide showing the two Newport bridges, the castle and the Dos iron and nail works beyond the railway bridge.

The Monmouthshire and Brecon Canal was the starting point. At last a route, albeit slow and circuitous, that would carry the products of the growing number of ironworks and thousands of tons of minerals from the newly formed coalfields to the water's edge.

The Waterloo Hotel at the gates of the Alexandra Docks.

Griffith Clothiers, one of Newport earliest companies.

The Griffiths staff at Newport station at the start of their annual outing, c. 1920. Note the columns behind the group in readiness for the station canopy to be erected on the central platform.

The Griffiths van. The photographer at the time has cleverly erased the background, which was quite common in commercial photography when the prime subject was the vehicle and the company name.

The Monmouthshire and Brecon Canal was considered one of the more profitable canals in the network. This pleasant form of travel was a massive improvement in the 'roads' of the times, which were often pitted rough cart tracks, where more loads were spilled than delivered. However, as with all things good, its life was limited as the railways soon poured into Newport from all directions.

The railways shadowed the canals, often running side by side. The Monmouthshire Canal Company became the Monmouthshire Canal and Railway, before eventually coming under the control of the GWR.

By the 1930s trade had all but ceased on the canal and the links with the old dock and the Potter Street locks had been filled in. The canal, or rather the remains, terminated just beyond Barrack Hill.

It could be said that from the late 1800s to the 1960s Newport was the perfect industrial storm. The river, the canal (until the 1930s), the Old Town Dock and the Alexandra Docks were all active. Railway lines permeated the streets, serving industries, factories and the numerous foundries to be found from the town centre to the docks.

The industrial growth can best be illustrated by comparison with the population growth. In 1801 the population of the town was 1,135, in 1851 it had risen to 20,279, and in 1881 to 35,382.

The docks and transport industries accounted for much of the Newport workforce, either directly or as a supporting role. Mine owners and shipping companies had agents, many of which were to be found in Dock Street.

Jesseman bridged the gap, operating both as a manufacturing and support company. They made the donkey jacket and industrial gloves, and supported local industry by supplying asbestos packing and V belting – tubes, rubber piping and stuff from another era. Rolls of heat-resistant packing materials and patterns were stored in the basements.

The junior staff would take newly formed asbestos packing joints and dredge them in a number of graphite mixtures. The George Street factory was a step into the past. As late as the 1960s a long Dickensian clerk sat at a lectern-style desk with a ledger and a scratchy pen, which he frequently dipped into a china ink pot. All that entered or left was dutifully recorded – including the staff!

Industrial archaeology from the Potter Street Lock, Newport. Now sited on the Fourteen Locks Canal Centre, High Cross.

Meanwhile, at the dock entrance the glove factory offered a terrifying insight into the rag trade. Raucous, fun-loving ladies teased and verbally dismantled the unsuspecting delivery man or errand boy to the point where they would rather boil their heads in oil than chance five minutes with the Jesseman girls!

Manufacturing came in a number of guises: that for industry and that for the consumer. The Dos Works of J. J. Cordes, a Spanish industrialist, manufactured a wide range of nails and fastenings. It was one of the earliest factories in Newport.

Lower Dock Street – once a commercial hub, lavish in elegant Victorian architecture. Pictured from the previous site of John Cashmore Ship Breakers.

W. Jesseman, established in 1874. There were three premises in Newport: George Street, Watch House Parade and Mill Parade, adjacent to the Transporter Bridge.

There were others who enjoyed a similar lineage. As previously mentioned, Griffith Clothiers was established in 1870. Not all of Newport's industries got the recognition they deserved.

ROBERT WYNN AND SON

Robert Wynn & Son, haulage contractor, were but one of those companies who made a massive contribution to the town's industrial heritage and were the innovators of many of today's heavy transport practices.

Thomas Wynn, who originated from Uffculme in Devonshire, was in the employ of the railways as a contract carriage cleaner at Newport High Street station. It became evident to him that there was a gap in the services from rail to customer's door, and also a lack of transportation of goods from the railway to customers in the Valleys. With this in mind, he set up a business as a carrier moving goods from Newport High Street directly to the customer. In addition, he established a connection with Star Flower Mills, an arrangement that lasted for nearly a 100 years until the mill's closure.

Over 200 horses were in operation at one point, resulting in their premises in Shaftesbury Street on the banks of the river being acquired. This had space, stables and some properties attached to it, which was used by the Wynn family as they needed to be close to their business.

An opportunity to enter timber extraction resulted in premises being opened in Mid Wales. Again, this was successful and saw many specialist vehicles being acquired and built by the Wynns themselves.

Steam power was introduced and worked alongside the horse fleet for many years. One of the most important innovations was the building of a 40-ton-capacity heavy trailer for moving equipment to the John Lysaght's steel works, which was then under construction. Lysaght's were eventually to employ over 3,000 staff. This was perhaps the start of the Wynn's Heavy Haulage division, of which we are familiar with most today.

As most of us remember Wynn's – the classic combination of a Pacific Heavy Tractor, a swan-necked trailer, pushed by a Diamond T. This was a daily sight in and around Newport. Both vehicles are of US Army Second World War stock.

The old stable block at Shaftesbury Street – Wynn's Heavy Haulage.

A massive stator is moved up Barrack Hill, once part of the wide-load route. Interestingly, it passes over the defunct Monmouthshire and Brecon Canal, from which Newport's modern industrial heritage began.

A steam Sentinel road locomotive, timber carriage and load pauses to take on water, perhaps.

The past meets the present. The elderly 1920s John Fowler steam locomotive is eased into its display case outside the Albany offices of Robert Wynn by a modern Scammel contractor. In this late 1970s picture are Mr John Wynn and the late Mr Arthur Matthews, both of whom shared infinite knowledge of the industry both old and new.

THE ALBANY STREET PHENOMENA

Whereas Dock Street and Commercial Road are linked geographically by name to the docks and commercial activities in Pillgwenlly, Albany Street was, in contrast, a lesser-known road in the Shaftesbury area, known as the Marshes. It runs closely to the Usk and the Crindau Pills, which in the past were identified on some early maps as the 'Malpas Dock'.

New faces in old hats: the buildings remain but the old Newport companies have left. Small industrial units now occupy the spaces where pots were once thrown, hot sugars poured over marbled slabs and massive loads once 'sailed' on their arduous journeys to places beyond imagination.

This was once the entrance to Crindau Garages, which by the early 1960s had become the home to Robert Wynn's.

Albany Street was reached via Lyne Road, which in turn branched off Shaftesbury Street. Shaftesbury and Crindau are among the older communities of the present city. Yes, it's all very confusing, as what we all know as Shaftesbury Street was originally named Marshes Road, which I assume came from the watery nature of the terrain.

Lyne Road and Albany Street is shown on the 1889 John's Street map, though I am unsure if Albany Street was adopted at that time. The interchange with Marshes Road and Albany Street came at the junction of Barrack Hill, which was in essence a crossroads, and also at the point where the railway crossed overhead in close vicinity to the early Marshes Turnpike Gate railway station.

Terraced houses soon showed their characteristic styles as new streets appeared in Shaftesbury, Henry and Hoskin Streets, and the blossoming area of Crindau was soon to follow. This offered a ready-made workforce to the new and growing industries on that side of the town.

The Crindau Gas Works were opened in 1885, as was the Crindau Glass Works – glass workers' cottages are still in evidence. Albany Street and its small web of interlocking thoroughfares never really stole the historic limelight as it did the more prominent areas of Pill, Baneswell and Maindee. It was, however, home to some of Newport's oldest business. Places of work that offered employment to hundreds of Newport families.

There was Crindau Gas Works, Crindau Glass Works and Robert Wynn (Crindau Garages), which, when they later when moved from Shaftesbury Street, became their main depot.

Other local industries included G. F Lovells, confectioners, known also for their popular cafés and works football team. The Newport Pottery and the Mole Grip was another claim to fame – Newport 'was the Home of The Mole Wrench'. In addition, Ansell's Brewery had a bottling plant, and there was of course the much-loved Coronation Club. There were others too, some light engineering and plant hire, and the printing works.

Newport grew from a muddy marsh to a thriving business community in just a few decades – an unsung chapter in the city's story of work.

The disused Crindau Gas Works as it was in the late 1980s.

A sweet favourite manufactured in Newport.

The popular Lovell's Café – a must after a day's shopping.

THE OTHER SIDE OF THE FENCE

Newport's heartlands were built on marshes, most of which were below sea level in the years of the Industrial Revolution. When the houses came they were terraced – some with two storeys, others with a basement. Many fell down owing to the speed of their construction and had to be rebuilt or, in some cases, have the ground around them raised to support the walls.

The long lines of sentry-type dwellings were the city walls, but in many cases it was what lay behind those walls that was integral to the workforce in the community. Built in block formations, row upon row, almost like a trusted military square, they housed hundreds of families, many of which were large or extended. That was the way. But within those symmetrical confines there existed a plethora of businesses and workspaces, which varied in range from a garden shed to a small factory.

The variation was immense: ice cream produced in an old boiler, a brass foundry, a soft drinks factory, a laundry. They were often hard to find as there were no neon signs, only perhaps a faded wooden board. This was sometimes hand-written, showing faded lettering, the handiwork of another artisan of the streets – the sign writer. There were, however, pointers. Arched doors often led the way to a stable, the local milk man or the coal man. Other strange apertures were a mere side entrance to the casual eye, but were in fact entranceways.

To the sole trader the backyard was his storage. His slates were neatly stacked (you couldn't afford to smash too many Welsh slates) and were the tools of their trade. There were strange shapes covered in tarpaulin and old hessian sacking – not much to the gaze of the outsider, but integral to the work in hand.

Between the rows, backstreet garages and workshops are clearly seen in this partially redeveloped image of Charlotte Street.

The terraced street – workers' homes at the heart of the community.

Shed store or factory? The potential was endless to the entrepreneurial terraced dweller.

The typical mid-terrace arch – at this time a garage, but historically the home of Vile Bros, the soft drinks factory.

74, ALMA STREET,

Newport, Mon., July 4th 1928

Miss Parry

Dr. to Miss B. England,

DRESSMAKER & COSTUMIER.

Icons of a family butcher. Behind the shop there was once an early slaughterhouse. *Inset*: From Miss England, dressmaker of Alma Street.

NEWPORT AND THE AMERICAN CIVIL WAR

One of the most bizarre and intriguing tales to arrive from this look at working life in Newport came from the Southern Skirmish Group, who I can assure is not a Pillgwenlly street militia or a bowls team! It is a group who closely follow the history of the American Civil War. Their fascinating story came to my attention through the Pill Heritage Centre via the late Mr Bill Miles of the Newport U3A.

The northern states of America, the Union, had thrown a blockade around the Confederacy. This caused massive disruption to the cotton trade, of which many northern cities in Britain relied upon. It was imperative that both imports and exports continued as they were essential to the commerce of the south and also to the war effort. Britain was responsible for the construction of many fast ships, which became known as the blockade runners. Built here and sometimes registered in France, they sneaked past the Union warships and when apprehended could use their speed to break out and reach their destination. Records show that one of the more famous, the *Alalbama*, was frequently in Britain and indeed came to Newport.

During one such visit of a blockade runner, the ship's captain ventured into Newport in search of a sympathetic man of the cloth who might donate Bibles for the troops on the front line. This happened and crates of the good book were sent to Newport Docks to be loaded aboard the blockade runner.

It was during the process of winching the crates aboard that the accident happened. The net containing the Bibles slipped and the crate crashed to the ground, spilling the contents over the dock side.

Each Bible had been hollowed out and the space filled with musket balls for the Confederate army. These lead munitions had been forged in the backstreet sheds of Pillgwenlly. Newport's first cottage industries.

The ports of Newport and Bristol exported high-quality paper from the Cheddar paper mills. This was used by the Confederate states as bank notes, as many of their own paper manufacturing facilities were destroyed during the conflict. In 1996 a Newport furniture restorer found a Confederate bank note in an old chair he was restoring. This note is now on display in the Virginia State Museum.

An early hand-coloured lantern slide of the *Lightning* crossing the Atlantic.

All day police and militia have been securing the docks and the outlying area of the docks. At about midnight tonight the biggest cargo of explosives ever shipped by rail will arrive at the docks. Under the orders of the Chief of Police, Inspector Summerhayes, all lights are to be put out around the dock area, and this rule will be strictly enforced. The biggest fear of the Police is that of explosion. They say if this were to happen it would blow Newport out into the Channel.

Monmouthshire Merlin, 12 September 1863

A report in a *Monmouthshire Merlin* edition in September 1863 tells of two local women who appeared in court after having been found in a state of physical and mental disrepair while circumnavigating Dock Street. The ladies, who were suffering from rubber legs, no doubt after a night on the gin, were celebrating after one discovered that her brother who had left Newport to fight in the American Civil War was alive and well after being captured. They were fined 3s.

A May 1863 edition of the *Merlin* states that the southern vessel *Earlstow* was unloading a cargo of cotton, which was good news for the people of Manchester. This was a period of subterfuge and intrigue. Shipping carried large cargos of railway lines, ammunition and coal, destined for the southern states. All of which appeared to be closely linked with France, who have always had a strong connection to that region of America.

A mixture of sail and steam at Newport.

Possible evidence of Newport's connection to the Confederate States. A similar banknote was found in an old chair.

Ladies' committees operated a sewing and knitting group for the southern troops, making balaclavas and stockings. This was accompanied by tin mugs, false limbs and other locally made artefacts on the circuitous route to the southern states taken by the blockade runners.

Evidence suggests that the militant and self-willed dockers of Newport and South Wales were making up their own minds as opposed to the national stance on the American Civil War.

THE END OF THE INDUSTRIAL REVOLUTION

As the years of the Industrial Revolution drew to a close, the end of the canal as a working partner in Newport's history drew nearer. There were reports of disused narrowboats being stockpiled, rotting away, and extensions into the lower reaches of the town were being clawed back.

Newport had become a vibrant centre of commerce and industry. The river, the docks and the land mass, now fully reclaimed, became as one. In 1871, the *Tredegar Boat*, the first trading boat on the river, struck disaster. It was just before Christmas when the heavily laden boat floundered near the mouth of the river. Lives were lost; it was a disaster. Shortly after that event another boat was put on station that belonged to one Mr Kemeys. His charges for passengers and freight were considerably less than the *Tredegar Boat* and the service became known as the Moderation Boat, which in turn became the Moderator Boat using the Moderator Wharf, of which we are all familiar.

Newport came of age during a period of rapid industrial growth. Any reference to the 'Fishing Village' had been assigned to history. Salmon fishing, however, would continue for many years with a limited number of licenced boats operating from the river and the dock.

One of Newport's boatmen, John Perkings, pictured in 1971.

Industry on the east bank ended at the Town Bridge, but here we see fishing boats resting on the banks in wait for the next tide.

THE TWENTIETH CENTURY

t is said that where there is muck there is brass, and the same sentiment also applies to war. For many years there was an armaments factory at Caerwent on the outskirts of the city. The Caerwent Royal Navy Propellant Factory was a highly secretive establishment, which in recent years, prior to closure, was in the hands of the Americans. This I can confirm, as one who was arrested while taking photographs of the site for a national newspaper. A scary day followed where I was in the hands of six well-armed GIs in an underground office with lights shining on my face, being questioned as to a possible Eastern European connection – oops.

This was the rail link to the national network. Munitions were regularly shipped from Newport Docks – as recent as 1990 and the Gulf Wars. Articulated vehicles lined the walls of the North Dock in Mill Parade, waiting to load their destructive cargo aboard American ships. The dock, as it remains now, was closed to the public. It was on such an occasion that I posed as a fisherman to see what was happening, only to find a large armed American guard smoking a huge cigar. His foot was resting on a sign saying, 'Danger Live Ammunition'!

The two world wars applied a new twist to the story of work in Newport. In the day of the earliest tram roads, which were little more than crude tutted tracks, women drove the mules that carried the ore and iron from the hillside foundry to the waiting canal boats. Now, again, the heavy responsibility of survival was on their shoulders as the men were sent to the Western Front and the families who remained were left fighting for their own survival.

While some women were able to enter munitions work, there were many with large families and mainly unsupported who were living on their wits and the help from within their immediate communities.

Fighting for one's country was a duty, but at the end of the day it was also work; it was a paid job. Sadly, with every job there is a downside, and for those who were left at home the downside was the lack of immediate money and the knowledge that he who was away fighting may not even be alive. The gruesome statistics gathering in France and on the Western Front endorsed this belief in the most horrendous manner.

Poverty was extreme. There was no welfare state and the age of the giro was many decades away. Illegal moneylenders operated from street corners. One well-known personality was nicknamed 'Quicksilver'. His weekly appearance in the terraced streets often meant the difference between food and rent or destitution. For many others, there was the unthinkable.

Containers customised our work styles, taking the work out of the skilled hands of our dockers. Here we see a loaded container vessel heading into the river to the Bell Ferry terminal.

The weighbridge at Newport Docks c. 1970, standing at the entrance to the Shell oil depot – more hazardous commodities on the edge of the community.

Newport munitions girls of the First World War.

In the First World War this large corner building in Alexandra Road was a crèche for munitions workers.

THE WORLD'S OLDEST PROFESSION

There can be no doubt that prostitution is the oldest form of paid work; a service industry where supply and demand never falters. Newport's back-to-back slums that were to be found in Friars Fields, behind Commercial Street, were renowned for its ladies of pleasure.

> A man trap. Hell's half acre. 'denizens and smiling nymphs, grinning inanely, waiting to pounce on the unsuspecting traveller who might have strayed the few yards from the principal Thorofare, Nanny Baulch, Mary the Cripple and the Duchess awaits your pleasure. Along with your watch, wallet and boots should one be mad enough to remove them, This was Friars Fields the "vile Rookery" a Badly drained plague spot'.

I know a few popular holiday destinations meeting that criteria.

Some years ago I interviewed a delightful lady who was approaching ninety-five years of age. I am unable to name the lady for obvious reasons; however, she told me the story of how her family coped during the harrowing years of the First World War:

> I had to leave school at the very earliest age. Father was sent to the front, and mother was at home with my six sisters. They were all too little to work and we had no money to speak of. Sometimes we helped out in the local shop. Mother sewed and repaired cloths for people. It was never enough. But my relatives, the older cousins, worked on the docks. Not dockers, they were prostitutes! But there was no shame in it, we had no money, nothing to live on. There were the moneylenders who came to the street, but that is another story. And when the war was over, they all found ordinary jobs and never went on the dock again.

She went on to make a very forceful and controversial statement to end the interview: 'Nobody knows poverty like we had then. The second war? That wasn't hardship, they were sissies!'

Above: You won't see Mary 'the Cripple' or 'the Duchess', but you might get a job in one of the numerous new restaurants or cinemas now occupying Friars Fields.

Right: The Victorian gin house, the haunt of ladies supplying pleasures of the flesh – at a price of course.

Two of the original safety posters by Newport artist Jack Clarke (inset).

WAR WORK

The period between the wars was a relatively short but eventful span in time. The Depression of the 1930s was a period when everything went into reverse: the economy, stock markets and the lack food production in the USA were just a few of the reasons behind those hard years. Men queued for a day's work. It was almost an auction, as the employers could have the pick of the bunch from the lines of hungry men.

Despite being named the war to end all wars, few, if any, lessons were learned. It was as if the great nations were only stopping for breath. In September 1939 it began again, and with even more ferocity than before.

Newport had broadened its industry, as the major works turned their efforts into munitions. There was money to be made. Many housewives resented family responsibilities and were anxious to get into the well-paid, though hard, work.

The ordnance factory in Corporation Road was opened as Newport went into wartime mode. The steel plant of John Lysaght equipped an underground hospital. It had first-aid facilities and a full operating theatre. It is said that the docks were so full of shipping that one could walk from one side of the dock to the other on the decks of the ships then moored.

Preparing for war must have generated huge incomes for factories, workers and suppliers, and at the other end of the spectrum, the black marketeers.

Work and wartime can be a strange and potent cocktail. While many men returning home found it difficult to adjust, the same can be said about those women who worked in the munitions industry. Well-paid work brought freedoms that were hard to relinquish when hostilities ceased.

Normal jobs did not just disappear at wartime; they were adapted to the circumstances of the day. Jack Clarke was an accomplished artist who worked in most medias. He was born in Commercial Road in 1901, but lived for many years in London where he exhibited his work at numerous venues. By trade he was a commercial artist, who during the hostilities became part of the ministry for information and produced stunning posters for the workplace. Pictured here are two of the original works and possibly the only picture of Jack, who eventually became publicity manager at Messrs Santon switch gear.

Munitions workers from the box factory, pictured in Constable Lane.

Uskside Engineering – another tank rolls off the production line.

At the end of hostilities, Field Marshall Montgomery joins a parade through the centre, passing shops whose names have stood the test of time (e.g. Stead & Simpson) and became an integral part of the local economy.

(Courtesy of Gareth Witt)

Trade in wartime Newport Docks and on the river was massive. Here is a picture of the early power station on the east bank of the Usk, its chimneys heavily camouflaged. Note the stockpile of coal.

Munition workers of the box factory.

Not every household enjoyed the benefits of the work in munitions or were involved in the shady dealings of the black marketeers. Hardship was commonplace when the breadwinner was away for sometimes years at a time. This rent book from a property on Malpas Road in 1943 clearly illustrates the willingness to pay, but not always meeting the agreed figure, which resulted in ongoing arears. (Name and address not shown on request.)

WORK AFTER WAR

It could also be said that the 1950s and 1960s were a time when jobs were easy to come by, and most of the industries founded in the late 1800s were still active in some form. Newport's housing estates were expanding rapidly too. The system of terraced housing, which still prevailed, was a rich source of manpower for small businesses. Those small traders in the community knew who was about to leave the education system and would be available for work. All that was needed was to ask the question 'Are you working, do you want a job?'

They may have not been quality jobs and there were companies that always had a high turnover of staff, owing to the nature of the work. There were, however, opportunities with smaller concerns for apprenticeships, which for many were a great starting point to a career.

The armed services and the railways were still recruiting – surprising as the railways were soon to be the subject of a massive reorganisation under Dr Richard Beeching.

Many jobs were still gained through families – if Dad worked there, the son was also employed. This was the case with the docks and also in some of the major iron- and steel-manufacturing companies. These were the old ways when longevity in employment was the norm.

Local terraced housing.

Mr Alan Brown receives an award for fifty years' service with Robert Wynn & Sons from Mr H. P. Wynn in 1955. It is said that Alan, as a boy, walked horses from their Somerset farm to Newport for the growing fleet of horse-drawn vehicles then used by the firm. He stayed and continued service with the company until the 1960s. At least eight of the Brown family served the company from early 1900 until the firm moved from their hometown in the 1980s.

CHEERS! MAKE MINE A PINT

Throughout time brewing has played a major part in the town's history of work. Pubs and inns greatly outweighed the population, and in recent years Newport has often been referred to as one of the country's most drunken cities. No less than twelve breweries were listed in the 1882 trade directory. Hancock's, Castle Breweries, Anchor Breweries, Lloyds and Yorath and Phillips were among the larger and earliest companies. Many of these were lost to the larger concerns such as Ansell's Courage and Bass Charrington. Brains is still a popular beer, though brewed in Cardiff, a mere 12 miles away.

A young Gemma Preece 'can't wait to taste her first pint of Lloyd's'.

Now occupied by the George Street warehouse, Phillips still maintain a presence, albeit just signage that states they were brewers and wine merchants. This was their stables. It would be good to know how many horses were operated in the town in those heady days of growth.

Both Hancock's and Mitchell and Butlers were big names in the town's brewing history, as were Courage and Ansell. The twentieth-century Newport dweller was never far from a brewery or bottling plant. There was a plethora of such establishments in the Pill area of the town, all of which employed many people, and had imposing buildings.

Courage beers were adjacent to the cattle market – all the breweries were central to a distribution point. As a publicity exercise the Courage horse-drawn dray often made an appearance – a magnificent sight delivering once again to the streets of Newport.

The Courage shires were stabled at the Northernhay Stud, near the Altyryn stretch of the canal. Who could possibly not like the use of horses as a means of work, bringing home the beer and the bread, the milk and the scrap man? Coal for the stove and a more than generous little offering to go on the roses, free of charge.

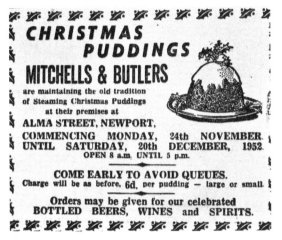

Right: The *Hancock's Magazine* of July 1926.

Hancock's staff of the same year.

T. E. SHELL, C. ROLLS, R. WATTS, J. LONG, H. BURNETT, P. COLLINS, FRED VILLIS, JIM VILLIS, G. CHAPMAN, N. EVANS. THE WHOLE OF THE STAFF, DRIVERS AND BOTTLERS, ETC., EMPLOYED IN THE BOTTLING DEPARTMENT, WHEN MR. SHELL TOOK OVER THE MANAGEMENT IN 1902.

Thatcher's Brewery, Mountjoy, Newport. It was to here that the annual Christmas pudding pilgrimage took place with beautifully home-made puddings, cooked in the steam from the bottling plant.

Staff at the Hancock's Brewery, Alma Street, enjoy a pint with the retiring Mr William Spencer, manager at the plant.

Mr William Spencer, Hancock's Brewery.

Known as the Anchor Brewery, this large complex was situated between Cardiff Road and Alma Street, including part of Pell's Lane.

The Courage
offices in Lower
Dock Street,
adjacent to the
cattle market. Also
visible is the Dock
Street station
goods depot.

Shire horses
for pulling
the Courage
dray, stabled
in Newport.

The Maltings,
the Old Town
Dock – only the
walls survive today,
following a fire.

FOOD AND DRINK

Most fish and chip shops never required a huge staff as they were often family concerns, with the owners living above the shop. As a rule, they were never really known for their architectural qualities; it was what went on behind the counter that provided the magic.

Those who have survived the passing years have had to diversify to stay afloat. Perhaps the last bastion of the traditional fish and chips were Johns in Cardiff Road and Shepheards of Maesglas, who are still producing world-class fish and chips.

Husband and wife teams, with perhaps one or two part-time staff, hardly made an impact on work statistics, but taken as a whole they were an important part in the small business sector. So should those men of old who wrestled with the name of our ancient borough, as it was then, have called it the 'Chip Shop Village'?

A definite hierarchy existed in the land of battered cod, but it was a simple equation to arrive at the correct conclusion: an empty chippy was not using the right dripping.

Among the many food outlets that have contributed to Newport's economy, there were to be found two that one could consider special. Lovell's, known for their 'Milky Lunch', boiled sweets and local cafés, and Pell's, established in Newport many years ago, famous throughout for their mint humbugs.

I can unashamedly say that a walk down Pell's Lane, leading into Cardiff Road, was a sensory hell. Hops from the brewery, sugary, sweet and unctuous slabs of flavoured boiled sugar from Pell's Yard and a torturous wisp of hot pies from the nearby Blaenavon bakery.

A Victorian lantern slide depicting street vendors.

Angy's Fish Bar, Commercial Road. We all have our memories of the 'chippie'. The great Sir Winston Churchill refused to add fish and chips to the list of wartime rationed foods as it was considered a food of happiness and morale boosting.

In the 1960s and 1970s there were a number of mobile fish vans operating in the town, frequently seen wherever there was a street gathering or fête. Often a conversion, the stovepipe chimney belching out fishy-flavoured fumes stated their presence long before they entered one's street.

THE STORY OF PELL'S

I had the great pleasure of knowing the late Mr Arthur Pell, who gave me valuable information about the 'Old Firm', as he called it. They originated, as so many of Newport's commercial icons, in Pillgwenlly. James Pell was born in 1799 and lived and traded as a baker and boiled sweet confectioner in Bolt Street. In later years they moved to their well-known premises in Commercial Road with a shopfront and a rear workshop making bread and cakes.

They employed ten male craftsman, who remained until the late 1950s. They were primarily known for their confectionary, though the majority of their trade came from fresh bread and cakes, which could be eaten immediately from the oven or from many retail outlets in Newport and the Valleys. The transport in the early days were by horse and cart. Polly was known as Newport's most mettlesome pony, who would kick her rear legs in anger when under pressure. The mornings were cake deliveries and the afternoons were sweets delivered to the Valleys. It is said that the famous Pell's Old English Mints, known as Pell's Black-Drops, could be smelt across the pews in the myriad of chapels in the mining towns of the valleys. A favourite to suck during the lengthy sermons.

Pell's appeared in the Newport provisions market. They supplied cakes and confectionery to many of the major high street stores in the area, including Marks & Spencer, Hills and Steels and Woolworths.

There were other excursions into tearooms, but it was the myriad of small shops found in the town's terraced streets that provided the backbone of the business.

A small team of craftsmen served the firm for many years. Pell's survived early financial uncertainty following the death of the founder, but it was expertly managed back to strength. Two world wars, the Depression and the General Strike failed to dent their popularity.

Pell's Lane and the rear of Pell's Confectioners.

Post Polly, a modern addition to the transport department, pictured in Conway Road.

Adding colour and flavour to sugar boiling at the Pell's factory.

In the late 1950s it was decided to move from the old buildings in Commercial Road to a new factory in Conway Road. Here they added modern packaging equipment, which they would use to wrap and distribute their many lines of sweets and confectionary.

While Pell's were the popularist sweet, G. F. Lovell, who were also confectioners and bakers, traded in a larger and more national capacity. Their trademark 'Rexville' became a password for the famous Lovell's toffee.

Many of the Lovell's athletic soccer players were picked out by Newport County AFC. One notable and popular player was striker Roddy Jones.

Sweet making was a popular cottage industry, though often hampered by rationing, as was the case of the Second World War. There were others, such as Charles Berry in Church Road, and Christopher's in Pill. Sweet making was, in many cases, a back-kitchen industry – small quantities for a select clientele of neighbours and those in the immediate community.

Paid work came at a premium as outside factors influenced the availability and quality of work. The Depression of the 1930s and the General Strike were two events that seriously impacted Newport's industry. In the hardest of times, men queued each day for a few hours' work. The companies that were running had the pick of the crop at whatever rate they wished to pay.

At the new premises at Conway Road, modern machinery gave Pell's their claim to fame: they were the first British company who could successfully wrap the Pear Drop.

Humbugs by the shovelful, Conway Road.

KEEP FIT

by eating

LOVELL'S TOFFEE REX

The King of Toffees

•

SOLD EVERYWHERE

•

G. F. Lovell & Co. Ltd., Rexville, Newport, Mon., Swansea and Manchester

One 'kept fit' by eating the famous chewy sweet, enjoying the pleasures of the High Street Tea Rooms. If you were super fit you might be trialled for their Welsh League soccer team.

Rod Jones (back row, second from left), former Lovells Athletic footballer, at the Newport County AFC Player of the Year Awards.

N E W P O R T

I N D U S T R I A L   C O U N C I L   C E N T R A L   S T R I K E

C O M M I T T E E.

OFFICIAL BULLETIN No. 8.   FRIDAY 14TH MAY, 1926.

WHAT THE SETTLEMENT MEANS.

THE GENERAL COUNCIL'S ATTITUDE.

The General Council called off the General Strike in confidence that the Prime Minister meant what he said when he asked for resumption of negotiations towards an honourable peace.
Peace depends upon employers abstaining from attempts of victimisation. It depends upon their declining to follow the example some are setting of using this position to attack the position of Trade Unionism.
Their effect will be that the unions, for self-protection will be compelled to offer the most stubborn resistance.
The whole purpose expressed by the Prime Minister will be null and void if this occurs.
The Government, if it means what the Prime Minister said, must stop this attack on Trade Unionism. It must demand that the employers abstain from victimisation.
Unless this obligation is fulfilled the Trade Unions will have no alternative but to resist to the uttermost.
Their resistive capacity is unimpaired. They cannot tolerate the imposition of conditions which attempt their destruction.
The good faith of the Prime Minister is involved. A peace without vindictiveness is impossible unless this attack ceases. A vindictive peace only means a new strength. We need acts and not words if work is to be resumed. The workers will not surrender their hard-won gains of many years. The Government has said it does not desire this. Let it act firmly and quickly to that end.

A letter to the trade unions relating to the General Strike, Friday 14 May 1926.

THE DOCKERS, THE SHIPBUILDERS AND THE STEELMAKERS

Engineering and the docks were, without doubt, the bedrock of local trade and provided work for many thousands of Newport families.

The Old Town Dock closed between the wars, leaving the river wharves and the Alexandra Dock to provide the shipping outlets to the town. The ground that had been gained when the old dock was filled in was soon occupied by engineering and scrap-metal companies. Many of the dockside buildings assumed new identities.

A. R. Adams' home (boiler maker) was in Court-y-Bella Terrace, where they enjoyed a rail link to the adjacent docks branch in addition to a large yard that held a fascinating array of small saddle tank locomotives. However, the prestigious refurbishment of the ex-GWR locomotive King George V was carried out on land that was once the Old Town Dock, then the United Wagon Works.

In 1906 a link was established between the lower reaches of the Usk and the east and west banks, following the opening of the Transporter Bridge. Industry on the east bank was galvanised by the huge steel mills of John Lysaght's, Monsanto and Stewarts and Lloyds.

Mrs. TUCKER,

VINE COTTAGE,

COMMERCIAL ROAD,

~ NEWPORT.

𝕎𝕒𝕤𝕙𝕚𝕟𝕘 & 𝕄𝕖𝕟𝕕𝕚𝕟𝕘 𝕕𝕠𝕟𝕖 𝕗𝕠𝕣 ℂ𝕒𝕡𝕥𝕒𝕚𝕟𝕤 𝕒𝕟𝕕 𝕆𝕗𝕗𝕚𝕔𝕖𝕣𝕤.

The small business spin-offs were many, as seen by Mrs Tucker's offer to captains and officers for washing and mending.

The imposing backdrop of the *Sunflower E*, set against thousands of tons of imported coal, Alexandra North Dock.

Copper-capped magnificence, a Swindon masterpiece brought back to life by a Newport workforce of skilled craftsman and engineers.

The Newport Dock Police Force, the British Transport Police of 1944 – challenging times!

Coal trimmers of the United National Colliery Company, probably pictured on one of the many coal hoists, *c.* 1920. Many of the wharfs on the River Usk belonged to the mining companies.

John Lysaght Iron and Steel. The Lliswerry Pill can just be seen at the top left of the picture.

JOHN LYSAGHT, LIMITED

MEN ON SERVICE
IN THE WAR
AND
ROLL OF HONOUR
1914

BRISTOL, NEWPORT, SCUNTHORPE, WOLVERHAMPTON.

Such were the high losses of Newport personnel in the First World War it is believed that further editions of the roll of honour booklet were discontinued.

The opening of the Transporter Bridge provided easy access from the Pillgwenlly bank to the east bank.

The control tower at Stephenson Road.

The tug *John Lawrence* moving a steam crane between the Old Tow Docks and the Alexandra Dock. It is pictured passing under the Transporter Bridge c. 1930.

This Smith and Rodley mobile crane was a regular visitor to the Alexandra Dock. Cranes like this were used to dismantle the railway system after the great Dr Beeching breakdown of the national system.

Men of the Isca Foundry, 1909. These were part of the team that built the new lock gates.

For the new lock entrance at Newport Docks. History created in chalk!

This was liklely a sand boat for Messrs Sessions. These boats were regular visitors to the river for many decades.

The Bristolian. Small tankers served the Shell oil depot and were regular visitors to Newport.

Water floods into the new dock here in 1907. Scenes such as this are once-in-a-lifetime images.

An empty sea lock with the trappings of construction littering the banks, 1912.

The sea lock in 2015, no longer open to the public.

As the South Wales Coalfield slowly died, the question was often asked 'Why are we importing coal, when we have the finest steam coal in the world literally under our feet?'

Above: What a difference a few years make. The Tredegar Dry Docks closed in the late 1960s and were filled in. A number of transport packaging companies occupied the building, such as Cyprian Fox. Here we see the lock entrance about to be sealed forever, as the new road was fast approaching.

Right: Newport has a number of graving docks suitable for ship repair and fitting out. Here we see the *Manzanares*. Looking at the ragged plimsole line, she is enjoying a coat of paint.

NEW SHIPBUILDING IN NEWPORT

In 1953 a new company appeared on the south dock called the Atlantic Shipbuilding Company and employed over 250 personnel. It had a chequered history, but in its short life produced a number of fine vessels.

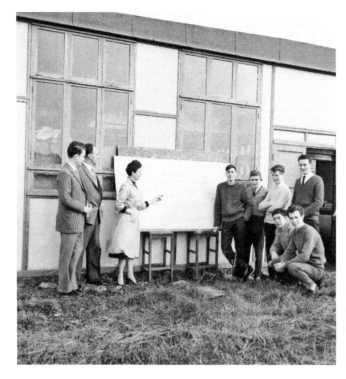

The beginnings of a new project: a team of young employees inspect the working blueprints of a new vessel.

The Habana awaits its launch, with the crowded quayside and the popping champagne bottles are not far away. A number of the Atlantic boats were to work on the Great Lakes in North America.

The Newport skyline tells the story of work: cranes, ships, super structures and wisps of smoke against grey skies. In the far left is the Transporter Bridge, while on deck are oxyacetylene bottles, cables and a large concrete weight, probably used to keep the ships plates in place during welding.

Not much going on here, but the two figures below the jib of the rail-mounted crane indicate the size of the undertaking.

Taken from the flooded lock, soon to be taken from the yards to the dock for the final fitting out.

Not long before sea trials, the fitting-out process is well underway in the Alexandra Dock. The part-completed ships were moved by tugs into the docks for the final works.

THE GREAT WORKS

So many of Newport's workplaces were at the water's edge. Perhaps the biggest employer in Newport, in terms of staff and subsidiary companies, was the Massive Llanwern steel plant. This was originally Richard Thomas and Baldwins. It opened in 1962, but for years the construction caused chaos to Newport's transport infrastructure as hundreds of shale lorries (tippers) moved around the crowded town. Such were the numbers that when a wagon was finally worn out they were often buried under the mass of infill required to fill the marshy Gwent levels upon which it was built.

Established in 1835, Cordes (Dos Works) is Newport's oldest foundry. Why did a Spanish industrialist choose Newport, I wonder?

The Cordes works buildings is now listed.

The Lysaght's jetty under construction. Across the river is the entrance to the Old Town Dock and a tantalising look at a mixture of steam and sail.

A comparative newcomer to the Newport work scene, the company began life in Tredegar in 1903. It opened its continuous strip loop here in Courtybella, Newport, in the early 1920s.

Another of the city's oldest engineering companies: Uskside iron and steel works. It was situated in a truncated Church Street, which at one time ran down to the Old Town Dock.

The horizon is filled with the massive Llanwern plant, dwarfing the rolling mill of John Lysaghts in the foreground. In recent years the plant was savagely downgraded, losing 3,000 jobs when the steel-making heavy end was closed in favour of the Port Talbot works.

When the heavy end of the massive Llanwern steel works closed, the components of the furnaces were shipped from Newport to Port Talbot for further use. Pictured here, they enter the Alexandra North Dock in a convoy of huge loads.

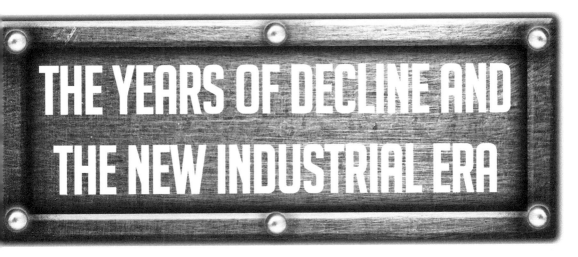

THE YEARS OF DECLINE AND THE NEW INDUSTRIAL ERA

Perhaps it was a coincidence that they sounded the death knell for Pill at a time when the writing was on the wall for the old ways. I use the term 'old ways' unashamedly and with affection, as it was for many of us the ways of our world. Be they good or bad. The rise of the council estate, the reservation for the thousands of those who were, by slight of pen, plunged into slums and depravation loomed on the horizon. Slowly but surely the river lost its traffic, as the steel plants and shipbreakers succumbed to the changing times.

Decay remained for many years after the decline in industry and the Pill redevelopment.

Scaffolding, dereliction and architectural despair at the junction of Lower Dock Street and George Street. Happily, this area was destined to become a conservation area.

Blaina Wharf, they called it, the Jacks Pill trading estate. It was, of course, Cashmore's and the haunt of other notable names such as Mordey and Carney.

Unwanted steam locomotives once lined this area in readiness for the breaker's torch. On the opposite side of the wall, the great liners met their eventual fate.

Above: The workplaces here were never replaced. It stood empty for many years, until recently when new houses were constructed as part of a major regeneration of the city and its surroundings.

Right: A delightful relief of the great Queen Victoria, daubed in paint, probably from a spray can, looking less like a Banksy and more like a Bankruptcy! More work for the demolition men as the building eventually burned to the ground.

In the 1980s, the town centre entered a new stage. The Kingsway Centre had been built and was a damp squib as far as most traders were concerned. The new inner ring was still under 'regeneration'.

The river, which was once an ever-important highway of trade and work opportunity, might well have been dry, as the last vestiges of trade rumbled on.

Despite the huge upheaval in the city, Newport has never lost its connection to shipbreaking. Here on the North Dock, taken in the late 1990s, a ship is broken on the quayside, resulting in some highly unusual photographs.

There is not much of this left to cut up on the North Dock. The Gaer estate is sprawled across the horizon, an award-winning council development built in the 1950s. Scrap metal continues to play a major part in the story of work in Newport. In recent years a massive scrap shredder, said to be the largest in the world, was installed in Newport Docks by Sim's Metals.

The local shop and local traders were hit hard by the conditions. The front room emporium virtually ceased to exist, as the terraced rows tumbled and the supermarkets took the land of the industries, and in doing so, offering a new type of work opportunity.

It might have had flaking paint and it was probably a hotbed of gossip, But where in those far-off days would one get a pint of milk at 2 a.m.?

The era of the supermarket had clearly arrived. J. Sainsbury then occupied what was once Wynn's, the cold store, the slaughterhouse and other retail outlets.

Phillips and Sons, brewers and maltsters. This fine building was used for car auctions in the 1980s.

The twilight years on the Usk. The last few jetties to work, one of which was Bowater's. Blaenau Wharf in the distance was used by the Campbell's boat for a short time.

The low river bridge, built as part of the docks ring road, prevents the use of any sizeable vessel in the upper reaches. When they built the bridge, the original old trading highway, Newport's historic commercial lifeline serving the city, the borough and the village died – RIP.

Perhaps one of the saddest forms of work to vanish in that period was that of the small trader – the coalman, the milkman and the weekly collectors. The coalman's lot was not a happy one. It was great when the streets were flat and a short carry to the coal shed or cupboard under the stairs were all that was required. However, homes had a nasty habit of having steps, and the early council flats on Newport's estates were initially built with coal fires. This left the long-suffering coalie to often climb three flights with a heavy sack on his shoulder.

FINANCIAL SERVICES

There is one aspect in our story of work in Newport that has been a constant down the ages, and that is financial services. Though it has always been there, it has hugely changed its identity to stay in touch with modern technology.

Life insurance was a much-revered necessity in a day when the payments were left behind the clock on the mantelpiece and the agent came to the house with the pay-out. Mike Lewis began his career in 1968 with Pearl Assurance. Previously, many of his family had worked for Cashmore's. His rounds were varied and in all parts of the town; however, he says that his favourite was, without doubt, in Pill. He recalls with affection the system of dealing with his clients' needs – the collections and the paying out when people sadly passed on. A professional in the field of insurance and finance, he tells of the other side: the community interaction that he as a 'collector' enjoyed. How he advised on the new wallpaper, filled the coal bucket, helped the elderly with shopping, helped fill out tax returns and carried messages from one family member to another.

His work clearly had social implications, especially for the elderly who had been customers for most of their working lives. At that time there were penny and even halfpenny policies, which were to be dealt with as decimalisation loomed.

By the nature of his work he had to assume a responsible and professional attitude, but after moving to the head office in Peterborough, where he was a training officer, he retired and was able to relate his anecdotal experiences, which border on the hysterical.

'The call came that Dad had at last left this world. I collected the policies and the pay out which was then made in cash to the client, and made the visit. The gentleman in question was on the table as many were at that time. Having made the correct overtures I was about to hand over the money when the person in question moved!'

'He is not dead'

'Yes but he is nearly gone,' came the reply. 'It won't be much longer!'

I gathered the pay-out together and left the house. Shortly after that the call came again. This time he had in fact left us.

When I had settled and drank the customary cup of bereavement tea, I was about to leave when the relative called me to one side and said, 'I don't suppose you want to buy these, only wore them once.' 'She was offering me his boots!' All in a day's work for the insurance man.

As the demolition of Pill continued and the concept of telephone sales grew, his round in Pill came to an end. The final death knell for the 'man on the knocker' was the internet and the call centre. Baneswell was the next on the list, as a route was sought for the inner relief road.

Stone and aggregate has always played a part in the story of work. Quarries and brick works were in St Julian's, Barrack Hill, High Cross and Malpas. Most have now gone, but the demand for railway ballast is ongoing and the quarry at Machen on the Newport boundary is still active.

Above left: Machen Quarry supplying ballast to the rail industry.

Above right: Mr Mike Lewis, representative for Pearl Assurance.

═ INSURANCE INDUSTRY ═
UNEMPLOYMENT INSURANCE SCHEME
(GREAT BRITAIN AND NORTHERN IRELAND).
Unemployment Insurance Act, 1920, Section 18.

Certificate of Insurance
AGAINST UNEMPLOYMENT

This is to certify that the holder of this Certificate

Harold K. Jones

....
(NAME OF INSURED PERSON)

Agent

Occupation .. .. ..

6 Capel Crescent, Newport.

An early certificate of insurance against unemployment.

There is a lane – a secret lane – in which there is a garage. This same lane remained unnoticed for years. The small garage was often father-and-son-based work. The son was perhaps apprenticed or maybe just learned the trade by being hands on. The prevailing smell of paint thinners, oils and grease was an acrid but pleasant experience. Sadly missed.

Happily much public opinion and second thoughts spared the charming old area of Baneswell a similar pain to Pill.

THE FUTURE – A NEW GENERATION AND A NEW STYLE OF WORK BECKONS

A study of the historic Lower Dock Street would surely unlock the true history of Newport and those who lived and worked here. It is not so active now the shipping agents and the embassies have left. However, the future looks sound for this thoroughfare as the magic words 'preservation' and 'regeneration' are frequently heard. After two previous attempts had failed, Newport gained city status in 2002. After number of years of hiding the cracks, Newport now has that city feeling.

This brings more work for the building and construction industries as the mountains of red brick and random stone is cleared in preparation for the new generation of industries.

Newport has many small independent companies specialising in all manner of commodities. One in particular belonged to Geoff Watkins, an entrepreneur whose business was based on the use of vintage cars for social and corporate occasions.

Newport has never completely lost touch with its work heritage. The plethora of breweries – Hancock's, Mitchell and Butler, etc. – have been replaced with a number of distribution depots. While dozens of old-style pubs have closed for whatever reason, with some becoming restaurants. There has emerged a number of first-class microbreweries. Perhaps brewing history is about to repeat itself.

It is the arts, the service industries and education that the city has now taken to its heart.

Like so many other things that we once called a 'rock' the Church has undergone a period of uncertainty. More and more people are looking for answers in other areas, which has left many old buildings with Mr and Mrs Uncertainty in their congregation. These buildings, which were expensive to maintain from their conception, have not suffered the passing of time gladly. St Barnabas, off George Street, closed many years ago and was in the hands of Central Press for a long period. When they closed it was quickly snapped up by Jan Martin, a lady who could be best described as a friend to the city.

Lower Dock Street.

Mariners Quay – an appropriate name as this row bordered the Old Town Dock to the right and John Cashmore's shipbreakers to the left.

With few local shops remaining careers in retail are met by the major retailers and the supermarkets. Miles of railway track that once served the massive dock and river complex of wharves have been lifted for scrap, and much of the ground is now occupied by the ubiquitous industrial estate.

Geoff Watkins restoring a 1927 Daimler.

The Riverfront Arts Centre, a futuristic kilner jar, preserving what might just be a graveyard for more medieval ships.

The Barnabas Arts House, New Ruperra Street.

Now to speak of the artist. With craft workshops and inexpensive studio space to rent, and exhibition space, the Barnbas Art House will move into the future along with modernity as a place to work, view and appreciate.

I believe the changing face of Newport was first seen with the arrival of the statistics office from London. Initially staffed with a nucleus staff from the city, it is now a pivotal employer in and outside of the city. A number of successful high-tech industries have come to the city, along with call centres and financial services. In recent years Admiral have taken a prime position in the centre adjacent to the railway station.

Elegance, sophistication and style, the Barnabas Arts House founded by Jan Martin.

The Admiral building, imposing against the snail-like station building.

The regeneration of the centre has transformed the feel of a city, in name only, to a vibrant 'we are going somewhere' community. Bringing the university campus to the riverbank makes further education an environmentally pleasant location. Perhaps a few boats or a ferry up to the delights of Caerleon would enhance the experience further.

Cleppa Park on the outskirts of Newport seems to have been the chosen site for the new technologies. Panasonic were one of the original companies, yet it was when the giant LG Electronics arrived in 1996 and committed to a massive semi-conductor plant that there was much anticipation of a new and vibrant work era, which would eventually create over 6,000 jobs.

The Newport Campus.

The Newport Campus – now called the Student Village.

The same building under construction a few years earlier. The austere concrete of the George Street Bridge *c.* 1964 makes it look grubby. Add some colour to modern architecture and it makes it less boring.

This image is of the interior of the Uskside Engineering Works, formerly Uskside Iron and Steel. They were formed in the early 1820s and were still here in Newport, as Newelco, 162 years later.

Split-level development for retail and leisure, and a mixture of themed eating places.

Still standing after all these years! And still producing their famous home-made chips and traditional thick curry sauce – so thick you can stand a fork in it.

The habit of having food and drink on every corner is a far cry from the plethora of hot dog stalls that used to trade in the centre. All of the major supermarkets have refreshment areas; one is never far from a burger or cheese butty.

The LG plant closed just a few years later, in 2006.

The most recent redevelopment of the Newport centre has brought a new dimension to both retail and leisure to the city. Big named stores and a host of themed restaurants, the like of which has not been before.

Much emphasis is placed on fast food in all cities, and Newport is no exception. With many pubs being snapped up and turned into take-out establishments, it is hard to find any originality.

In the 1960s there were few establishments selling curry or Chinese food as a main course. The Kismet in Clarence Place; the New Moon, a Chinese restaurant; and according to the 1960 Kelly's directory, a yet to be named restaurant in Charles Street belonging to Mr Ali. There is one, however, that has stood the test of time and is probably one of Newport's oldest Asian restaurants in the city. I refer, of course, to the Lahore.

At the other end of the spectrum and iconic to the city is the Celtic Manor. Fine dining, golf, gymnasia, fitness and leisure coupled with conference facilities that are still being enlarged, and accommodation, which has to date attracted the NATO conference and the prestigious Ryder Cup. Set in the grounds of the old Lydia Beynon Hospital, it is the icing on the cake as far as hospitality and outreach is to the new city.

There are many longstanding companies, large and small, that sadly I have had to omit. The cattle market and the Brattice cloth company, for example. All of which have made an outstanding contribution to Newport's industry.

Newport, the city, has sought new horizons and more strings to its bow, but as each decade passes, the skyline becomes less manageable to the naked eye.

The Celtic Manor resort, overlooking the city and the beautiful Usk Valley.

The Red Arrows fly low over the city in an impressive display celebrating the NATO conference held at the Celtic Manor.

It has been over forty years since I entered the workshops of Robert Wynn. Noise, heat, thick exhaust from the Cummins and Gardner engines. Multi-wheeled trailers, some with solid tyres, working then to their aged capacity. Yet, above all else it was the banter, the constant, often less than witty, exchange between men doing a hard and dirty job who were often away driving for three weeks at a time. The screaming tannoy and the incessant hammering and cutting of metals only added to the audible assault on the eardrums. Suitcases littered the office as travel warrants were issued and perhaps an advance on one's wages to pay for the digs. These are some of my most treasured memories.

Sainsbury's takes the spot occupied by the Crindau gas works, and the old yard and workshops now resemble a confusion of junk, stored goods, coaches, some trailers and an unoccupied snack bar. On mentioning my nostalgic interest, I was told to make the most of it as the site would soon be occupied by yet another supermarket. I won't go back.

Sunlight would make little difference to this extremely drab horizon. Perhaps it is best that it can only be seen from the upper floors of a multistorey car park.

A 365-degree turn shows a softer view of new houses lining the riverbank and a distant glimpse of Caerleon and the Usk Valley. I think if I had been designing the centre I would have had grass on the flat roofs.

A most pleasant part of the city is now seen. Hill Street, leading to the white-fronted Victoria Crescent, in which many skills were used in the preservation of this fine period terrace. The steeple of St Woolas Cathedral is just seen above the trees.

All new but for the river, mud and the ever-changing rush of the tide. It is a river, so where on earth are the boats?

The terraced street, the human warrens from whence came hardworking men and women – the butcher, the baker, the candlestick maker. Their rusting tools of trade now hang in disused garden sheds or dust-filled cardboard boxes, stored in equally inaccessible corners, shared only by the cadavers of ungainly dead garden spiders.

The modern port of Newport, automated and clean. Dockers no longer wait at the call stand for a day's work. But there is no such thing as an unskilled man or woman, for they who have spent their working lives at the helm of a sweeping brush do it because they are far better at that than you or I.

ACKNOWLEDGEMENTS

I have been involved both with heritage and with the Pill Heritage Centre for thirty years or more and in that time many people have, with great kindness, shared their lives and their stories with me through the medium of photography. Of these, many of whom do not wish to be mentioned, I thank profusely.

I have taken every effort to ascertain copyright and obtain permissions to use the enclosed images. In addition, I would like to especially thank the following for their input and help: Newport City Council, Mr Arthur Pell, Newport Museum Services, the late Mr Cliff Knight, Mr Duncan Brown, Mr Malcom Beardmore of A. R. Adams, Mr Ron Inglis (formerly Newport Library and Museum), Jan Preece picture library and heritage collection, Mr Don Carter, Gwent Family History, Mr Doug Parker, Uskside Engineering Company, Pill Heritage Centre, Newport Resource Centre Commercial Road, Mr John Wynn, Mr Jim Oniel, Jan Martin Barnabus Arts Cente, Mr Geoff Watkins, Mr Mike Lewis, Jake Cummins, Gemma Bullock.

Special thanks to Duncan Brown, who continues to amaze me with his knowledge and images of everything from a boundary post to a barley-twist drainpipe.